The Blacksmith in Eighteenth-Century Williamsburg

An Account of His Life & Times and of His Craft

Harold B. Gill

(Editor: Thomas K. Ford)

Alpha Editions

This edition published in 2021

ISBN : 9789355113078

Design and Setting By
Alpha Editions
www.alphaedis.com
Email - info@alphaedis.com

Contents

The Blacksmith in Eighteenth-Century Williamsburg

"Iron seemeth a simple metal, but in its nature are many mysteries," wrote Joseph Glanvill, a seventeenth-century English churchman. To the contrary, Henry Wadsworth Longfellow, two centuries later, found nothing mysterious about the worker in iron. His brawny blacksmith (long hair and all) embodied every simple virtue: he owed money to no man, prayed in church on Sundays, and earned an honest living by the sweat of his honest brow.

Longfellow may have realized that he was penning a swan song for the village blacksmith, whose forge and anvil could not last far into the factory age. Most probably, however, the poet did not think of himself as reducing to the level of small-town banality the lusty craftsman whose precursors forged thunderbolts for the gods.

To primitive peoples, it seems, there has always been something supernatural about the smith. He tamed fire to his will. He turned the ores of earth into magic and invincible weapons, or into prosaically peaceful tools. He himself became a god: Osiris of Egypt, Hephaestus to the ancient Greeks, Vulcan of Roman theology, Odin in Norse myth. Or he turned into a whole race of demigods—giant Cyclops or dwarf Nibelungs—having mystical skills in metalwork.

SEEKERS FOR GOLD AND IRON

Down through all recorded civilizations man has valued gold as the most precious of metals. Yet in every civilization since man learned to smelt and forge it, iron has in fact been the metal most valuable to him.

The paradox is more apparent than real. Iron is a common metal, and (with steel) can be put to an almost unlimited variety of uses—including the working of other metals. Its real value to man is utilitarian, although it may be employed for decorative and even monetary purposes. Gold, on the other hand, although of somewhat limited usefulness, is comparatively rare and is valued more for that than for its durable beauty.

It was, in part, the hope of finding gold—as the Spanish had found it in Mexico and Peru—that moved Sir Walter Raleigh to send colonizing ventures to North America. But any resource that might bring wealth to the gentlemen adventurers in London and to England itself was not to be overlooked. Thomas Hariot, one of those who reached Roanoke Island with Raleigh's initial colonists in 1585, reported that:

> In two places of the countrey specially, one about fourescore, & the other six score miles from the fort or place where we dwelt, we found nere the water side the ground to be rocky, which by the triall of a Minerall man was found to hold iron richly. It is found in many places of the country els.

Around the edges of a brass clock face made in England about 1750 and now in the possession of Colonial Williamsburg, some unknown engraver depicted ironworking operations. Here, above the numbers 11 and 12 on the clock face, open-pit miners are shown digging and hauling ore.

Nothing further is known of these discoveries, including their exact location, for the Roanoke colony did not survive. But the settlement made in 1607 at Jamestown did endure. Sending careful instructions, the sponsoring Virginia Company of London directed the adventurers to Virginia to look not only for gold but for iron ore. Among the first group of settlers was George Read, a blacksmith, to be joined the following year by Richard Dole of the same craft, and Peter Keffer, gunsmith.

No doubt some of these workers in iron—perhaps all three of them—had a hand in the experimental smelting and forging of local bog iron during Jamestown's first year or two. Captain John Smith reported that the colony's "best commoditie was Iron which we made into little chissels." Archaeological excavations at Jamestown and at nearby Denbigh Plantation in recent years have disclosed the sites of what appear to have been small furnaces for smelting iron ore.

At the same time, the colonists were shipping ore back to England, seven tons of iron being smelted at Bristol from Virginia ore as early as 1608. Four years later, William Strachey wrote:

> Sir Tho: Dale hath mencioned in his Letters to the [Worthies?] of the Councell of a goodly Iron myne, and Capt Newport hath brought home of that mettell so sufficient a tryall, as there hath bene made 16. or 17. tonne of Iron, so good as the East Indian Marchants bought that of the Virginian Company, preferring that before any other Iron of what Country soever.

A conjectural sketch, after Sidney King, of an earthen furnace for smelting iron. Furnaces such as this were used in England early in the seventeenth century, and similar ones may have been used at Jamestown.

In further pursuit of its determination to set up an iron industry in Virginia, the London Company advertised for blacksmiths, bellows makers, edgetool makers, cutlers, armorers, gunsmiths, iron miners, iron refiners, iron founders, hammermen, millwrights for iron mills, and colliers for charcoal making. Before the *Mayflower* left old Plymouth with its cargo of religious refugees, more than one hundred workmen having the required skills had sailed to Virginia, some of them to set up a full-scale ironworks at Falling Creek, about sixty miles up the James River from Jamestown.

How much iron was actually produced at the Falling Creek furnace and forge, whether largely pig iron, sow iron, or wrought iron, and whether consumed in the colony, shipped to England, or some of both, must remain matters of conjecture. A series of troubles plagued the project, but by 1619 the blast furnace, finery, forge, and chafery were reported to be "in some good forwardnesse, and a proofe is sent of *Iron* made there." Two years later a new manager was sent over, and he promised "to finish the Works & have plentiful provision of Iron ... by next Easter."

The forecast was fateful. Easter in 1622 fell on March 24. But on the morning of Good Friday, March 22, the Indians of Virginia fell on every English settlement along the James River, massacring more than 350 colonists, including 27 at Falling Creek. The redskins not only slaughtered the entire adult complement of ironworkers, but destroyed the buildings and supposedly heaved some of the machinery into the river nearby. The exact details are understandably a little vague, but the result was conclusive: the iron industry in Virginia was ended for nearly one hundred years.

EARLY IRONMASTERS

Except for bloomeries, which could have existed in every colony, the first successful ironworks in British America began production about 1645 at Saugus, Massachusetts. (In a bloomery operation a lump of iron ore—usually bog iron—is heated until it is semimolten, and then is hammered on the anvil until most impurities have been forced out; with much labor in this manner, small quantities of excellent wrought iron can be produced.) The Saugus works have been reconstructed after careful archaeological and historical research; a sort of family resemblance is to be presumed between them and the ironworks built in Virginia early in the eighteenth century.

The Hammersmith ironworks on the Saugus River in Massachusetts as they are believed to have looked in 1650. Along with documentary records, extensive remains found below ground at the site—and some above—have permitted a careful rebuilding of the entire complex. Redrawn after an architectural rendering in the Saugus Museum.

Governor Alexander Spotswood re-launched the iron industry in Virginia with the financial backing of several gentlemen in the colony and in England, and with the skilled labor of immigrant ironworkers from Germany. By 1718 it appears that his Tubal works, near the confluence of the Rapidan and Rappahannock rivers, were in production, although he had not yet received the London government's permission even to start the project.

Fourteen years later Spotswood (by then out of office) told William Byrd II of Westover that iron mines and blast furnaces were operating at four locations in Virginia. Byrd visited and described those at Tubal, not far from Germanna, at Fredericksville, and at Massaponax (now called New Post) below Fredericksburg. Spotswood had an interest in the second, and was sole proprietor of the first and third, having bought out his original backers.

The fourth was at Accokeek, near the Potomac, on land belonging to Augustine Washington, whose son George had just been born. Byrd, who did not get that far on his 1732 "Progress to the Mines," nevertheless confidently reported that "Matters are very well managed there, and no expense is spared to make them profitable, which is not the case in the works I have already mentioned." This judgment may have been accurate for all we know, but it seems unkind of Byrd to throw the only bouquet to the one place he had not seen while dropping brickbats on the men who had been so hospitable and helpful to him.

His criticism was certainly well founded in one case. The furnace at Fredericksville (a place no longer on the map) had been idle the entire summer. Somewhat like the rider who was lost for want of a horseshoe nail, here the blast furnace could not operate even though ore, limestone, charcoal, waterpower, and skilled labor were all available. The missing "nail" in this case was corn. There was not enough to feed the oxen that hauled the carts that carried the ore from mine to furnace and the sows from furnace to dockside on the Rappahannock some twenty-four miles away.

Byrd, who had a notion to become an ironmaster himself, was advised that a proper works required, besides an iron deposit nearby, a constant supply of waterpower to operate the bellows, easy access to deep water for shipping the output to England, at least two miles square of woodland to supply charcoal for a "moderate" furnace, and 120 slaves to do the work, including some to grow food for both men and beasts. Two bits of advice, which he recorded as follows, may have dissuaded him from taking the plunge:

> If all these circumstances happily concur, and you could procure honest colliers and firemen, which will be difficult to do....

> The founders find it very hot work to tend the furnace, especially in summer, and are obliged to spend no small part of their earnings in strong drink to recruit their spirits.

Spotswood's Tubal works were producing, in 1723, castiron "backs and frames for Chymmes [chimneys], Potts, doggs, frying, stewing and baking pans." But even at the time of Byrd's trip, the output of the four Virginia furnaces consisted almost entirely of cast iron sows and pigs that were shipped to England. There was not a single forge operating in the whole of Virginia, Spotswood told Byrd.

Just three years later, however, Governor William Gooch reported to the Board of Trade in London that one forge was producing bar iron. He seemed to think this was enough to satisfy the colony's needs for iron "for agriculture and Planting, for mending as well as making tools." How badly Gooch misjudged the local demand for wrought iron is evident in the rapid increase of forges in the following years. A number sprang up near the lower Potomac and in the Shenandoah Valley; one, called Holt's Forge, was erected sometime before 1755 between Williamsburg and Richmond at what is now Providence Forge. Its output just before the Revolution included bar iron and such plantation supplies as plow hoes, broad hoes, hilling hoes, grubbing hoes with steel edges, nails, and axes.

Legally, no colonial forge with trip hammer, rolling mill to fashion wrought iron plate, or slitting mill to turn the plate into bars could be built after Parliament passed the Iron Act of 1750. But the law seems to have had little effect, and Virginia smiths called for more and more bar iron to make farm tools and ironwork for wagons, mills, and ships.

The demand was so great that most bar iron produced in the colonies was consumed by local blacksmiths. In 1764, for example, Colonel John Tayloe, who owned ironworks in King George County, found he could sell his whole output locally. Robert Carter, the planter-entrepreneur of Nomini Hall and partner in the Baltimore iron Works, sold large quantities of bar iron in Williamsburg and to blacksmiths elsewhere in Virginia.

By 1770 William Hunter's works at Falmouth, said to be the largest in America at that time, were turning one and one-half tons of pig iron into bars every day. In 1781 Thomas Jefferson, who had a small interest in three blast furnaces in his home county of Albermarle and who later owned a nail making machine and sold its output, counted eight ironworks in Virginia. He reported that they produced about 4,400 tons of pig iron and more than 900 tons of bar iron annually.

THE COUNTRY BLACKSMITH

Two blacksmiths and a gunsmith, as we have seen, came to Jamestown with the earliest settlers, recruited for the obvious reason that their crafts were vital to the survival of any settlement in the wilderness. From the start, both the London Company and the colonial assembly tried to persuade smiths to migrate, and, when they reached the New World, to practice their craft.

By way of encouragement, the assembly exempted from taxes and levies artisans who engaged in their crafts and did not plant tobacco. In 1657, in order to assure smiths, tanners, and weavers ample raw materials to work with, it forbade the exportation of iron, hides, and wool. This latter law had a checkered career: it was repealed the next year, reenacted two years later, repealed as a failure after eleven years, reenacted once more after another eleven years, and immediately repealed by royal order as a threat to the trade and commerce of England.

Through it all the supply of working smiths remained small in the colony of Virginia, and their charges skyrocketed. The county courts were given regulatory powers "by reason of the unconscionable rates, [that] smiths do exact on the inhabitants of this countrey for their worke." Later and for another reason—the runaway inflation that accompanied the Revolution—prices of many commodities were commonly fixed. For instance, the price of bar iron (a consumer item for smiths) was set by a Williamsburg town meeting of July 16, 1779, at 800 shillings per ton and eightpence per pound "for the present month."

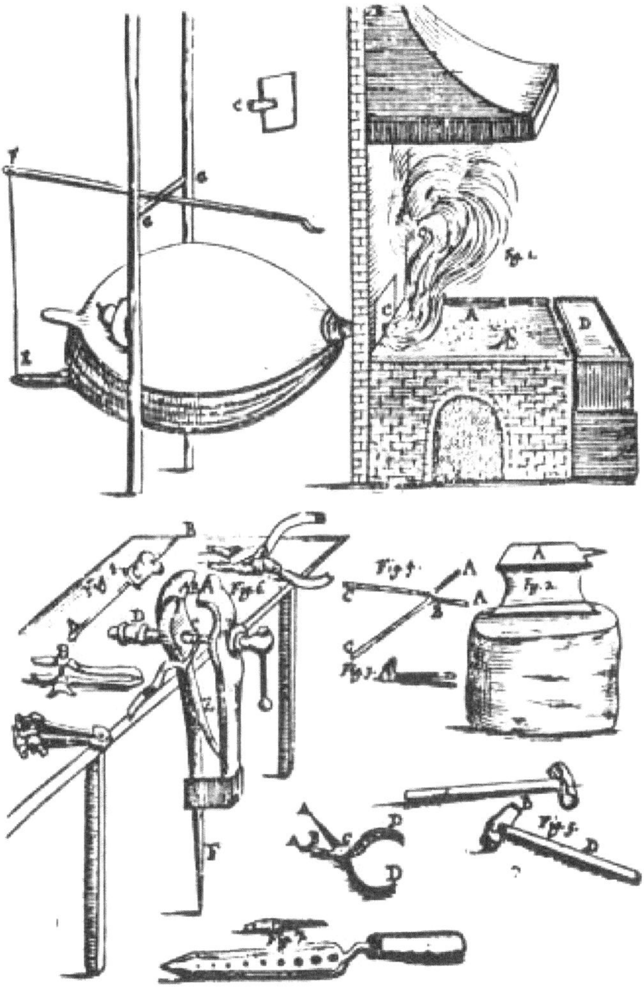

Shown in this illustration from Joseph Moxon's MECHANICK EXERCISES, *published in several eighteenth-century editions in London, are the basic pieces of equipment in a blacksmith's shop—then and since. Actually, the bellows connection shown is faulty: the draft must come up through the firebed, not blow across the top of it.*

Actually the greatest obstacles to the growth in seventeenth-century Virginia of any large manufactory of iron and steel articles were the scarcities of cash money and, even more simply, of towns. Hartwell, Blair, and Chilton, in their report to the London

Board of Trade, entitled *The Present State of Virginia, and the College*, described the situation in 1697:

> For want of Towns, Markets, and Money, there is but little Encouragement for Tradesmen and Artificers, and therefore little Choice of them, and their Labour very dear in the Country. A Tradesman having no Opportunity of a Market where he can buy Meat, Milk, Corn, and all other things, must either make Corn, keep Cows, and raise Stocks himself, or must ride about the Country to buy Meat and Corn where he can find it; and then is puzzled to find Carriers, Drovers, Butchers, Salting (for he can't buy one Joynt or two) and a great many other Things, which there would be no Occasion for, if there were Towns and Markets. Then a great deal of the Tradesman's Time being necessarily spent in going and coming to and from his Work, in dispers'd Country Plantations, and his Pay being generally in straggling Parcels of Tobacco, the Collection whereof costs about 10 per Cent. and the best of this Pay coming but once a Year, so that he cannot turn his Hand frequently with a small Stock, as Tradesmen do in England and elsewhere, all this occasions the Dearth of all Tradesmen's Labour, and likewise the Discouragement, Scarcity, and Insufficiency of Tradesmen.

When James Blair and his co-authors wrote of the difficulties faced by artificers, Williamsburg was about to be made the capital of the Virginia colony. Seventy years later Williamsburg was enjoying the height of its golden age—but the soil continued less than fertile for the growth of large-scale and urban iron workshops. Governor Fauquier reported to the board of Trade in 1766:

> There is but one manufactory of the least importance carried on in this Colony, which is, the making of Iron both in pigs and barrs, which receives no publick encouragement, and which when made is chiefly exported to Great Britain. But ... every gentleman of much property in land and negroes have some of their own negroes bred up in the trade of blacksmiths, and make axes, hoes, ploughshares, and such kind of coarse work for the use of their plantations. I do not know that there is a white-smith or maker of cutlery in the Colony.

Fauquier's report may be discounted as a politically motivated effort to allay the home government's suspicions that the colonists were engaging too heavily in iron manufacture. As a matter of fact, there was a whitesmith (that is, tinsmith or worker in white metal) by the name of John Bell in Williamsburg at the time Fauquier wrote. Records of the period mention cutlers at work in Williamsburg and elsewhere in the colony. But the point of paramount significance in his report lies in the undeniable fact that agricultural blacksmithing—and Virginia was an almost entirely agricultural colony—took place on the individual plantations. In addition to Negro slaves, some indentured servants, free journeymen, and master craftsmen—the latter occasionally itinerant—could be found working at their craft on farms throughout the colony.

Robert Carter, member of the council and sometime owner of a large home next to the Governor's Palace in Williamsburg, had workers on his plantations, white and black apparently, trained as coopers, carpenters, weavers, blacksmiths, millers, sailors, bricklayers, shoemakers, and in other skills. He sold iron articles made on his Nomini Hall plantation to his neighbors for cash or produce—such items as hoes, axes, plows, and nails. Although Carter was by no means typical, he being one of Virginia's wealthiest and most successful farm entrepreneurs, the example of plantation blacksmithing could be repeated many times over.

An instance of the availability of indentured servants is found in the 1773 advertisement of James Mills in the *Virginia Gazette*:

> JUST arrived the *Success's Increase*, Captain *Curtis*, with about eighty choice healthy Servants, among whom are many Tradesmen, viz. Shoemakers, Weavers, Carpenters, Black and White Smiths, Tailers, a Sailmaker, a Tanner, a Glazier and Painter, a Bricklayer, a Brass Founder, a Turner, an Upholsterer, Surgeons, and Apothecaries, Hair Dressers, Schoolmasters and Book-Keepers, with many Farmers, Labourers, &c. &c. The sale will commence at *Leeds* Town, on Monday the 3d of *January* and will continue till all are sold. Reasonable Credit will be allowed.... Tobacco will be taken in Payment for the above.

John Tait, another planter, wrote to England for a blacksmith who was "accustomed to coarse Country work," such as hoes and axes, to be indentured for four or five years and to receive £10 sterling per year in wages, plus "meat, drink, washing & lodging." Francis Jerdone, a planter and merchant of Louisa County, had an indentured servant who did all of the plantation's blacksmithing and also brought in as much £7 in one month of

1767 for work done for neighboring farmers. The following bill of John Cock indicates the kinds of work done by rural Virginia blacksmiths and the prices they charged in 1759:

	To making Niles and Shuing one whele	0	12	6
	To making a hoop one Staple and two Rings and Rivating the wheles by J. L.	0	5	6
1759				
January 4				
	To Shuing a pr of five foot and a half wheles and Rivating them Round A. L.	3	0	0
9	To making 5 Staples 1 Ring and 3 goosnecks	0	9	0
12	To making 5 Staples for the yokes & bees	0	4	0
	To making 3 hooks and 6 Rings	0	5	0
	To making 1 large Ring	0	1	0
	To making 8 small pins & Cuting a Chane and making a traces	0	3	6
20	To making 4 hooks and 4 Rings	0	4	0
	To making an ox chane	0	7	6
	To Lanthing an ox Chane and making a Staple and Ring	0	2	0
	To making a ploug Large	0	6	0
	To making an ax	0	2	0
F.1	To making three axes one of my iron	0	6	6
12	To Cuting a plough hoe	0	3	9
21	To Laying Eight hilling hoes	0	12	0
24	To Laying a fluck hoe of my iron	0	4	6

	To making a plough of my iron	0	10	0
	To making 3 hilling hoes	0	4	6
	To making 5 hilling hoes	0	7	6
		£8	10	9

THE VILLAGE BLACKSMITH

When the Virginia Assembly first met in 1699 at Middle Plantation (soon to be renamed Williamsburg), its members listened to speeches delivered by several students at the brand new College of William and Mary. Urging that the colony's capital should be moved thence from Jamestown, one of the students pointed out that Middle Plantation already contained "as many substantial housekeepers ... as is to be found again in the whole County." He specifically listed a smith's shop as one of several "great helps and advances made towards the beginning of a town."

Despite the young speaker's effort to make it sound impressive, Middle Plantation was far from being a town by any stretch of the word. But it was no accident that a mere scraggle of structures in a landscape of woods and fields included a smithy. As in the first years at Jamestown, the presence of a blacksmith to make and mend tools was essential to the success of the settlement. Unfortunately, nothing is known of the identity of that first Williamsburg smith—not his name, or the exact location of his shop, or the kind of work he did.

The Brush-Everard House is one of some eighty original structures now restored to their colonial appearance in Williamsburg.

John Brush was the earliest Williamsburg smith whose name is known today. He was primarily a gunsmith and armorer, but may have done blacksmithing too. He bought two lots in the shadow of the Governor's Palace in 1717, and the modest home he built there (later enlarged by Thomas Everard) still stands on Palace Green. So far as surviving records have revealed, he was followed by no more than fourteen individuals over the next three-quarters of a century who worked iron and steel in one or more of the smithy crafts: blacksmith, gunsmith, locksmith, cutler, nailmaker, and farrier.

Only fourteen. Even granting the possibility that some blacksmiths never left their name or mark in a written record, this seems remarkably few for so long a period in one of Virginia's chief towns. The small number can probably be taken as another indication that most of the colony's smiths—like eighty to ninety percent of its population—lived and worked in the country.

Surviving advertisements, invoices, and inventories of Williamsburg blacksmiths suggest that the work they did was of a somewhat different nature from that of the rural smith. The following extracts from account books of James Anderson and Thomas Pate indicate something of the urban variety:

1771	Mr. Henry Morse Dr to James Anderson				
Jan 22	To Cleaning 3 guns @ 3/	1	9	0	
March 22	To Cleaning 3 Do @ 3/	0	9	0	
August 28	To plating Chair Shafts	?	?	3	
	To mendg a spring	0	2	6	
1772					
May 25	To a New tumbler pr lock	0	2	6	
June 3	To Mending Bridle Bitt	0	0	7	½
7	To Mending a Chair	0	2	6	
July 30	To Altering a spring	0	3	9	
	To Do 2 bolts	0	1	3	

May 18	To feeding 2 horses 20 days @ 4/	4	0	0	
	To laing axletree pr Chair	0	15	0	
	To 3 Tiar Nails @ 1½d	0	0	4	½
	To pr Clamps pr Wheels	0	2	6	
July 5	To 2 gallons oats	0	1	3	
Decmb 7	To a key pr lock 2/6 mendg lock 1/3	0	3	9	
	....				
1774					
Jany 18	To a Nutt for Chair	0	0	7	½
Augt 22	To 8 Dog Nails 8d Cleang a Gun 2/6	0	3	2	
1775					
May 17	To a Key for a lock	0	2	6	
Work done for the Capitol By James Anderson					
1773					
May 24	To Cleaning a Stove	1	0	0	
July 26	To 4 Bars prs Statue	2	4	5	
Octr 3	To 3 Bars prl Doors @ 2/6	0	7	6	
	To 4 Do @ 5/ . 20 mendg a hinge 2/6	1	2	6	
4	To Eight hooks @ 7½	0	5	0	
15	To 2 Keys prs locks @ 3/9	0	7	6	
	To a Box prs do	0	1	6	
1773	Country Dr				
Apr 25	To half a Year Salary as Armourer to the Magazine £10				
1760	Collo Custis Estate to Thos Pate Dr.				

Feb. 11	To lenthening a Chain and mending a Bed pin for Cart	£0	3	0	
	To altering a Sett of Clamps Do	0	2	6	
19	To Pointing a Plough	0	2	6	
22	To Making a Screw key for the mill	0	2	6	
23	To Mending 2 Keys for Locks	0	2	6	
27	To Making 2 Bed pins and 2 Linch pins for Cart	0	6	3	
	To making Cleavey and Pin Do	0	3	9	
	To making Iron work for a Ox yoke	0	5	0	
March 5	To Making a Ox Chain	0	10	6	
	To making Iron Work for a Ox Yoke	0	3	9	
11	To Altering 3 Mill Hoops	0	3	9	
April 4	To mending a Lock and Key	0	2	0	
26	To Altring a Mill Spindle	0	5	0	
May 1	To Pointing a fluke hoe	0	2	6	
2	To Making 2 Wedges for the Mill	0	2	6	
7	To Mending a Sane	0	1	3	
30	To Pointing a fluke hoe	0	2	6	
June 3	To Dressing 3 mill Peaks and Lengthening a crane	0	5	0	
30	To Pointing a fluke hoe	0	2	6	
July 5	To Making a Hoope for Mill 10 pounds	0	7	8	
	To making 2 Wedges Do	0	2	6	
11	To mending a Broad Ax	0	1	3	
24	To mending a Key for a Lock	0	0	7	½
Novm 17	To making a box for a whip saw	0	3	9	

1761					
Feb. 3	To making 2 peed pins for Small Cart	0	2	6	
9	To Mending a Lock	0	1	3	

It will be noticed that Pate made or repaired several items "for the mill." No doubt this was the windmill shown on the "Frenchman's Map" of 1782 as standing on or near Custis's property to the south of town. The millwright, the wheelwright, the coachmaker, and the shipwright all depended heavily on the blacksmith to produce essential parts of their respective products. The builder of houses, too, could do little without the nails and the tools that came from the local smithy.

However, when the "public hospital, for persons of insane and disordered minds" was built in Williamsburg in 1771, the removable iron gratings and padlocks to be installed at all the windows were imported from England. For this large specialty job, even James Anderson, the town's foremost smith, was passed over. Similarly, wrought-iron gates and balconies on the public buildings of Williamsburg appear to have been ordered from England. The Capitol was to have "on each Side ... an Iron Balcony upon the first Floor," and the assembly explicitly empowered the overseers in charge of building both the first Capitol and the Governor's Palace to send to England for ironwork, glass, and other materials necessary.

Likewise, the elaborate gates at Westover plantation were made for William Byrd II in England. A "Set of Iron Palisades and Gates curiously wrought," sold as part of a prize cargo in Norfolk in 1748, probably came from France. When the House of Burgesses in 1768 commissioned a statue of the beloved Governor Botetourt, the sculptor, Richard Hayward of London, was also to provide the iron railing that surrounded the base of the statue when it was set up in the portico of the Capitol. One reason for importing ironwork for these large jobs may have been that local smiths were not equipped to handle them; more likely, the importation was politically wise since manufacturing in the colonies was discouraged by the British government.

Ornamental ironwork is less characteristic of the colonial Virginia scene than of Charleston, South Carolina, and New Orleans. Nevertheless, there are some survivals, none finer than these two gates at Westover plantation on the James River.

TOOLS AND TECHNIQUES

The bills and accounts quoted a few pages back, and others, give ample evidence that most colonial smiths could read and write—although their spelling (like George Washington's) might have a way of its own. At least one Williamsburg blacksmith, Hugh Orr, seems to have been quite a reader; at his death in 1764 he left a library of about forty books. But neither he nor any other colonial smith sat down to write out and illustrate a description of the work he did and how he did it.

This is not intended to be a how-to-do-it manual either. A few pages of text and pictures can hardly substitute for the apprenticeship of as much as seven years through which a blacksmith gained mastery of his craft. Only the close daily supervision of an expert and years of practice will enable a smith to know when the eye of his fire is large enough—but not too large ... when the forced draft of his bellows has made the fire hot enough—but not too hot ... when his iron is red enough—but not too red ... when his hammer blows fall heavily enough—but not too heavily to accomplish the particular job at hand.

Readers unfamiliar with the processes and products of a smithy are likely to be strangers also to many of the smith's tools—which makes for something of a problem in trying to describe them. For this and other reasons it seems wise to start with what may be the most familiar items today.

Nails. In the early years of the Jamestown colony land was plentiful and nails were scarce. They, like every other object of iron—except the "little chissels" mentioned by Captain John Smith—had to be brought over from England. When the soil of their tobacco fields was worn out, planters simply took up, cleared, and planted new land farther west. Sometimes they set fire to buildings on the abandoned land in order to salvage the nails for re-use, a practice that was forbidden by law in 1644.

However, nails were not difficult to make if one had a supply of wrought-iron rods and a few tools. Frontier farmers—which in eighteenth-century Virginia meant those living one or two hundred miles to the west of Williamsburg—sometimes spent winter days in nailmaking. The fireplace served as forge, and even the younger members of the family could wield tongs, hammers, and cold chisel or man the vise.

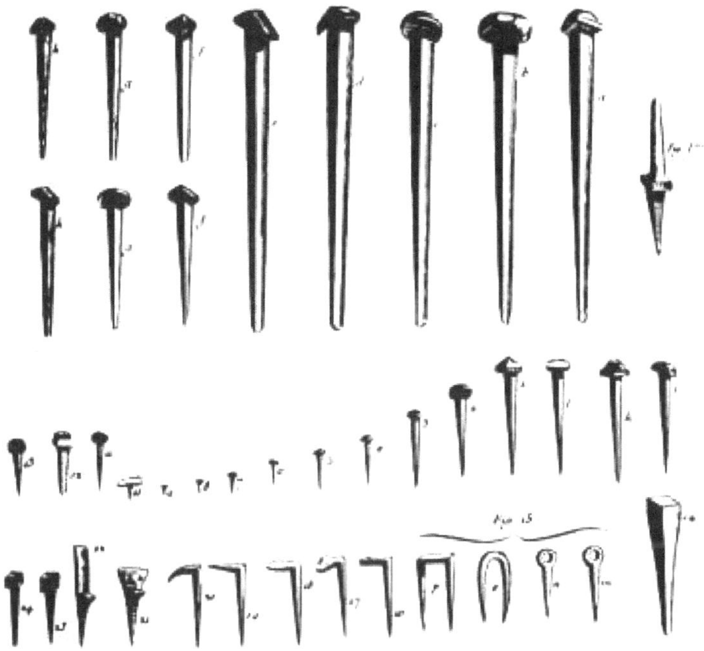

Nails and tacks of various sizes and shapes and for various special uses, from Diderot's encyclopedia. Figure 14 at the lower right is a wheel nail, for example.

Where there was a blacksmith, as we have already seen, he—or more likely his apprentice—made the nails. James Anderson estimated that eight boys could turn out twenty-five thousand nails in a week. Isaac Zane, who had an ironworks in the neighborhood of Winchester, owned "17 nailors tools great & small" and "2 nailors anvills." The smith probably started with iron several feet long, about one-quarter-inch in width and the same thickness, produced in a slitting mill. His first procedure was to draw them down—and here we come to the first terminological stumbling block. Drawing down (or drawing out or beating out) is the smith's phrase for thinning and lengthening a piece of metal by heating and hammering it. The contrary process of thickening—by hammering on the end of a rod—is called upsetting and is the technique used in making the head of the nail. Before he did that, though, the smith, having drawn down the rod to the proper thickness for the nails to be made, cut them to the desired length. Most likely he did this on a hardie, which is like a chisel held with the point upward in the square hardie hole of the anvil.

Horseshoes. Hugh Jones in 1724 wrote that horseshoes were "seldom used in the lower part of the country, where there are few stones." It is true that the soil of tidewater Virginia tends to be sandy and free of stones, so that horses could and did go unshod much of the time. Yet there is ample evidence—some of which we have seen in the accounts excerpted above—that blacksmiths and farriers worked in the Williamsburg area at making and mounting horseshoes.

The forge of Master Delafosse, royal farrier, in Paris in the mid-eighteenth century. From Diderot's encyclopedia.

A smith who made, fitted, and applied shoes to horses, mules, and oxen was properly called a farrier. The trade demands knowledge and skill in handling iron, and also knowledge and skill in handling the animals being shod. Because of his close familiarity with these animals, his "horse sense," so to speak, the farrier often served the function of veterinarian too. More often, however, it was the blacksmith who also served as farrier.

Horseshoes were made from bar iron, and they were normally custom made to fit not just a particular horse, but a particular one of his feet. Each shoe of a set of four will differ in one or more respects—size, shape, or weight—from its fellows, and each set may differ from others depending on the type of horse involved—draft, riding, carriage, etc.—and the condition of surface on which the shoes are to be used—ice, mud, stone, etc.

In addition, special shoes can correct defects in gait, guard against lameness, and the like. To describe how a smith made all of these possible variations is no part of this booklet. Suffice it to say that in the making of a horseshoe all of the blacksmith's basic tools come into use: forge, anvil, tongs, and vise. Some attention to each of these in turn will help to round out an understanding of the workings of the smithy.

Forge. The blacksmith's forge, which he sometimes calls his fire, is the most important feature of his shop. It consists of a square hearth, usually raised about two and one-half feet and made of brick, with a bellows at the side or back to blow the fire, a hood or hovel above to carry smoke and fumes away, and a trough or tub of water close by in which to quench the iron or cool the tongs.

The fire itself, of coal rather than charcoal, is always small and concentrated, a few inches across in the center of a hearth that may be four or five feet square. Around it lies unburnt fuel that the smith can handily bring closer when needed. With his slice—a long-handled, light-weight shovel—his fire-hook—a similarly long-handled rake—and his washer—a bunch of twigs to flick water around the fire—he carefully manages the size and depth of the fire. With the bellows he regulates its intensity.

The blacksmith must be able to judge when his stock is hot enough, and he does it by eye, the right degree of heat for a particular operation being revealed by the color of the iron. Blood-red heat is called for when the iron is not to be reshaped but only the surface to be smoothed. Flame heat or white heat is necessary when the work is to be hammered to a different shape, drawn down, or upset. Sparkling heat or welding heat is used only for the delicate and highly skilled process of welding.

Anvil. This is hardly less important to the smith than the forge, as he does practically all of his work on it. The common smith's anvil, made of cast or wrought iron, may weigh up to about three hundred pounds. It has had the same basic shape since ancient times, each of its features being functionally tried and perfected ages ago. The anvil's upper surface, called the face, is flat, smooth, so hard that a file will not cut it, and made of cast steel welded to the wrought iron body. One end of the anvil is a cone-shaped projection called the horn (also called beak, bick, bickern, or pike), used to work curved or rounded pieces of iron such as rings, links, or shackles. Between the horn and the face of the anvil is a small square area called the table. Its surface is not as hard as that of the face, and the smith places on it any work he wants to cut with a cold chisel. Near the other end or heel of the anvil are two holes, one round, called the pritchel hole, and the other square, called the hardie hole. When the smith intends to punch a hole through a piece of metal, he positions it over the pritchel hole so that the punch will pass into the hole rather than strike the face of the anvil. The hardie hole (also called the swage hole) is designed to take the square shanks of a variety of special-purpose bottom tools—which make their impact on the underside of the work when the smith strikes it from above.

Tongs. Iron being a metal that transmits heat readily, the blacksmith often cannot hold the piece he is working on, even with a gloved hand. He needs tongs to do the holding, and because of the differing shape of different objects being worked, he needs a variety of tongs of different shapes and sizes. These he ordinarily makes himself. John Brush of Williamsburg, for instance, owned "7 pair of Smiths Tongs."

Hammers. It has already been said that the smith's forge and anvil are among his essential tools. So is his hammer—or rather hammers, for he needs several of different shapes and weights, as well as a sledge or two.

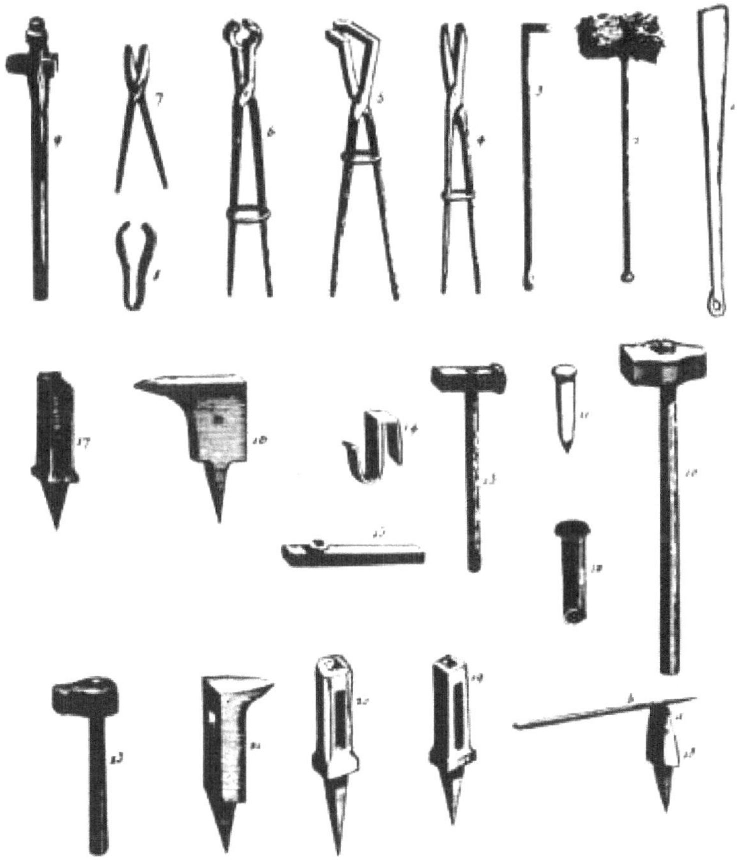

A small selection of tools such as would be found in almost any blacksmith's shop: fire tools, tongs, pincer, hammers, chisels, stamps, and stakes or hardies. From Diderot.

Vises. Smiths' vises are of two types, the large standing vise, used to hold iron for bending, riveting, filing, or polishing, and the small or hand vise to hold work of similar size. In both cases the work will have already undergone the major part of its forming on the anvil, and the vise comes into use almost solely for finishing operations.

Other tools that have particular uses may be no less important to the smith when he has occasion to use them. Among them may be mentioned drills, swages, swage blocks, hardies, stakes, punches, cold chisels, files, screw plates, flatter, fuller, header, and mandrel. It is recommended to the reader who wants to know the nature and uses of these and other tools in a smithy that he become an apprentice to the nearest blacksmith; there is no better way to learn.

Certainly no one can learn to anneal, braze, case-harden, temper, lay, and weld iron just by reading about it. But we can at least offer some definitions:

Annealing is the process of softening steel so that it can be worked by cutting tools. It is done by heating the piece in the fire to blood-red heat, then allowing it to cool slowly.

Brazing joins together two or more pieces of metal by the use of a brass solder, called spelter. It is used when the pieces to be joined are too thin to be welded.

Case hardening is the process of hardening the outer surfaces of iron or steel, while leaving the core soft and therefore tougher. According to Joseph Moxon's *Mechanick Exercises* (third edition published in London in 1703) it was to be accomplished as follows: Cover the iron all over with a cement made of powdered cow horn or hoof, coarse sea salt, stale urine or white wine vinegar, and clay, with more clay added to enclose the whole; when the clay has dried hard, put the whole lump in the fire and bring it to blood-red heat, no more; then take the iron out and quench it.

Tempering is the opposite of annealing, in that it slightly softens and toughens iron or steel. It is accomplished by bringing the object to the proper heat—which may differ according to the {...}

Laying was one of the most frequent operations performed by colonial smiths. Such implements as axes, hoes, and plows usually had wooden handles and wrought-iron heads, with a strip of steel welded on to make the cutting edge or face. When the last become worn, the process of replacing it was called laying or steeling.

Welding two pieces of iron is at the same time very simple in theory and very difficult in fact. At the proper heat the two pieces placed firmly face to face will—if the faces are clean—stick together without further ado. But accomplishing this feat requires great skill with the fire and great quickness with the hammer so that scale will not form on the surfaces to be welded. Normally the weld is hammered together on the anvil to refine the grain of the metal as it cools.

Another farrier's shop, no doubt drawn on the spot with tools and equipment just as they were seen by the artist. From Diderot.

THE ESSENTIAL CRAFT

James Anderson was described earlier in these pages as Williamsburg's foremost blacksmith during the years when his shop occupied a lot on Francis Street. Several of his ledger books are still in existence, some of them treasured possessions of Colonial Williamsburg. Among endless entries covering the laying of axes, hoes, plows, and colters, appear others that show the less routine aspects of Anderson's daily work: mending a poker; making a nut for a bolt of a chair (probably a riding chair); dressing two mill picks; mending a lock; altering 40 window hooks; making a hasp and staple for a henhouse; providing handle, wedges, and ring for a scythe; fixing a new end to an oyster clamp; putting a handle on a "teakittle"; forging a well chain; making a "strike tier," i.e., strakes for wagon wheel and nails to attach them; spindle for a wheel; prong for a dung fork; putting a hoop on a barrel; mending a coffee mill; 9 "fronts" and a rib for a griddle; 50 spikes; a pair of flatirons; mending and installing locks, keys, window bars, leg irons, and chains for the "lunatick hospital"; lengthening the bearer and adding a new middle foot to an andiron; "a Sett of Iron for a dressing table"; four breast plate buckles (for a harness); drilling a gun; mending an umbrella; "triming a horse feet"; making, mending, putting on, and taking off leg irons and hand cuffs for the jail.

Clearly everyone in town had to patronize the blacksmith sooner or later. He was, in a very real sense, a craftsman for all seasons.

THE BLACKSMITHS OF WILLIAMSBURG

This list includes only the men who were primarily blacksmiths or who clearly did blacksmithing along with their work in other iron crafts. The dates designate the years when they are known to have been in Williamsburg.

James Anderson, 1762-1798. Born in Gloucester County in 1740. Public armorer in Williamsburg from 1766, and supplier of arms to the Revolutionary forces of Virginia. His forge probably occupied the lot on Francis Street in Williamsburg next to the Barraud House. He employed a number of journeymen gunsmiths, blacksmiths, and nailers, and at one time had as many as nine apprentices. He and his shops were moved to Richmond along with other government agencies when that city became the seat of government in 1780; in 1793 he turned his Richmond shop over to his son and moved back to Williamsburg.

William Ashburn, 1774. Advertised in April of that year that he had opened shop near the Capitol in Williamsburg. May have been in town three years earlier, but little else is known of him.

John Bell, 1753-1776. Called himself both whitesmith and blacksmith. Served as public armorer from 1763 to 1766, when he moved to Portsmouth.

James Bird, 1740-1758. Established his shop "in the Market Square" on land leased from the trustees of the city of Williamsburg. Was lacking both as master and as businessman: an apprentice sued in court and obtained release from his indenture; pleading that the blacksmith "misused" him, and after his creditors foreclosed the mortgage on his property, Bird departed town "in low Circumstances."

Robert Bond, 1761-1783. Learned blacksmithing as an apprentice in Yorktown. Bought large quantities of bar iron from Robert Carter. Worked for the state during the Revolution and got caught in a bureaucratic vise: when the British destroyed his bellows he could not, despite an order from the commissioner of war, obtain "any Lether With out the Money and i am in tylerly idle theay wont Let Me Draw any

Provisions because i ant at Work and i Cant Doe anything With out my Bellus."

John Brush, 1717-1726. Primarily a gunsmith; may also have engaged in the blacksmith's trade. Thought to have been a protégé of Governor Spotswood because he did "work and reparations about the Governors House," and built his home on the Palace Green nearby. Was keeper of the public arms and those of the governor; in 1723 petitioned the legislature (in vain) for an allowance "for his misfortune in being blown up and hurt in firing the Guns on his Majtys Birthday."

Thomas Cowles, 1772-1775. He was a patient of Dr. John M. Galt, bought bar iron from Robert Carter, and repaired the arms of "Capt. Lynes Compy of Minute Men." Nothing else is known of him.

John Draper, 1769-1789. Blacksmith, farrier, and veterinary, whose shop was on Duke of Gloucester Street and who lived on the corner of Francis and Waller streets "where the Old Play House lately stood." During the Revolution he made guns, rented out riding chairs, rode express, repaired arms, and supplied nails and shot.

James, David, and William Geddy, 1736-about 1780. James Geddy, gunsmith, father of David and William (also of James Geddy, Jr., the silversmith), established his shop in Williamsburg sometime before 1736; he died in 1744. He and two of his sons did cutlery work, brass casting, and iron founding as well as gunsmithing; the sons also purveyed rupture bands and a vermifuge for horses, and offered to cure "the most inveterate Pole-evils and Fistulas ... and all Diseases incident to Horses." During the Revolution William was paid for repairing arms and casting ball; he died in 1784.

John Moody, 1776-1779. Smith and farrier, from Philadelphia by way of Norfolk, advertised his shop near the church in 1776. Was paid on several occasions for shoeing horses, but little more is known of him before his death in 1779.

Hugh Orr, 1738-1764. Captain Orr called himself both blacksmith and "hammer man," and settled in Williamsburg by 1738. His house and smithy were on Duke of Gloucester Street. He may have acted as farrier, and either he or a slave trained to do so performed phlebotomy—bleeding. He served as armorer for the colony for three years and may have been an officer in the Williamsburg militia. He is buried in Bruton churchyard.

Thomas Pate, 1760-1814. Did blacksmith work for John Custis and Lord Botetourt among others, and repaired arms for Virginia troops during the Revolution. The location of his shop is not known, but his purchase of more than 3,000 pounds of bar iron from Robert Carter in 1773 alone indicates a lively trade.

William Willis (or *Willess*), 1768-1770. Came from Birmingham and opened his gunsmith and blacksmith shop "near the playhouse" and "below the Capitol," but soon moved to Norfolk.

Suggestions for Further Reading

Alex W. Bealer, *The Art of Blacksmithing.* rev. ed. New York, Funk and Wagnalls, 1976.

Garry Hogg, *Hammer & Tongs: Blacksmithery Down the Ages.* London, Hutchinson Co., 1964.

J. G. Holmstrom, *Modern Blacksmithing and Horseshoeing.* Chicago, F. J. Drake & Co., 1941.

John Jernberg, *Forging: Manual of Practical Instruction in Hand Forging of Wrought Iron....* Chicago, American Technical Society, 1917.

William Allyn Richards, *Forging of Iron and Steel.* New York, D. Van Nostrand Co., 1915.

F. W. Robins, *The Smith: The Traditions and Lore of an Ancient Craft.* London, Rider and Co., 1953.

H. R. Bradley Smith, *Blacksmiths' and Farriers' Tools at Shelburne Museum: A History of Their Development from Forge to Factory.* Shelburne, Vt., Shelburne Museum, 1966.

Albert H. Sonn, *Early American Wrought Iron.* New York, Charles Scribner's Sons, 1928.

Aldren A. Watson, *The Village Blacksmith.* New York, Thomas Y. Crowell Co., 1968.